DAVID M. PARSONS
NEW AND SELECTED POEMS

'77

For the students
of College Park High
in honor of their National
English Honor Society ~

Best wishes,

Doug Parsons

DAVID M. PARSONS
NEW AND SELECTED POEMS

TCU PRESS
FORT WORTH, TEXAS

TCU TEXAS POETS LAUREATE SERIES

April 22, 2014

Library of Congress Cataloging-in-Publication Data

Parsons, David M., 1943-
  New and selected poems / David M. Parsons.
     p. cm. -- (TCU Texas poets laureate series)
  ISBN 978-0-87565-395-2 (hardcover : alk. paper)
  I. Title. II. Series: TCU Texas poets laureate series.
  PS3566.A769A6 2012
  811'.54--dc23
                         2012014363

TCU Press
P. O. Box 298300
Fort Worth, Texas 76129
817.257.7822
http://www.prs.tcu.edu

To order books: 1.800.826.8911

Designed by fusion29
www.fusion29.com

WITH BOUNDLESS LOVE
FOR MY EXTRAORDINARY FAMILY
AND
MY TREASURED FAMILY
OF TEXAS FRIENDS

Books by David M. Parsons

Editing Sky
Color of Mourning
Feathering Deep

table of contents

III Poems from *Feathering Deep* (2011)

IV New Poems

Introduction

David M. Parsons: New and Selected Poems is the seventh in the Texas Poets Laureate
Series published by TCU Press. The first six books in this series, edited by Billy
Bob Hill, have established themselves as essential pieces of Texas poetic letters
in general and as invaluable contributions to the works of the Texas Poets Laureate
in particular. It is an honor to be asked to serve as the new editor for the contin-
uing series. And it is a special pleasure to begin my efforts writing the foreword
to a book by such a talented poet as Dave Parsons.

Tracing a writer's source of inspiration sometimes can be a challenging task.
But at least one of Parsons's wellsprings is clear enough: he had the fortunate
opportunity to be living in Austin, Texas, during the 1960s, during the period
of the civil rights movement, the age of unfettered expression, and—especially
important to the development of a poet—the beginning of the Austin music
scene. This was the era of Rusty Wier, Michael Martin Murphey, Joe Ely, Jerry
Jeff Walker, among so many others. Those culture-shaping melodies and lyrics
could only have originated in Austin. There are multiple poems in this fine
collection that draw on both older and newer versions of Austin. "Good Friday,"
"Canoeing," "Austin Fire," and "Night Hawk" are just a few of the poems worth
returning to. Many of the street and place names mentioned in the lines will be
instantly recognizable to someone familiar with the area—but Parsons's talent is
such that the Central Texas setting, while adding texture to the poem, is only an
element in a larger message. Consider these lines from "Two Dogs Howling at
the Moon," a tribute to Rusty Wier.

and the thousands

of songs poured out like manna to the many hungering
audiences of the nightlife you so loved and I remember

at that moment thinking how Li Po is said to have so
adored that great luminous orb that he perished, when

after a night of heavy drinking, he fell into the lake
attempting to embrace the dazzling antediluvian body, tumbling

headlong and alone into the deep ink of oblivion,
or perhaps, the masked reflections of an eternal light

and how you, after sailing through countless gigs
and seas of agave, one complimentary shot at a time,

were now arduously floundering to make the best of each
of these last painfully clumsy egregious moments,

like you always have, with that distinctive dancing
twinkle in the weathered squint of those smiling blue

eyes, eyes still fully alive in my memory, still dancing—

I suppose every human passion holds within its core
the germ of something lethal to its being and yet,

somehow, interwoven with the potential of rapture.

Parsons's poetry, though, certainly is not limited to references about Austin and the music scene. He joined the US Marine Corps Reserve right after high school, and that military experience laid an indelible impression on his work. The poem "Re-Resurrection" is especially moving as it follows a stream-of-consciousness pathway that leads the poet, and reader, back to grief.

There are other poems in this collection that are worth attending—but for different reasons. Parsons believes in the pursuit of what Lorca called the *duende*, the spirit that allows us to reach for those ideas that are normally beyond reach. He believes that something should be at stake in the poem, there should be an idea worth reaching for, and that somewhere within a poem is a transformative moment. The poem "Feathering Deep" mentions this force specifically, but also it is echoed in these transformative and illuminating lines from the poem "Archaic Reflection ons Blake's Baptism."

. . .

Your last glimpse in rising might have been
the peaceful floating down of the dove,

but coming up and out and through the night
with a clutch of honed arrows, keen and quivered
gold, your sight wound round the tree of the font

to the end of the devilish curl, and it is there
where the head of a snaked darkness unfurled,
your mental flight surely must have sprung.

There are several influences at work in Parsons's poetry. These include James Dickey, Ted Hughes, Richard Wilbur, and Walt Whitman. In fact, two poems in this collection reference Ted Hughes in particular. These lines are from the poem "The Marriage Lost".

. . . a drumming heart—a catch of breath—still singing the sweet

turbulent tones

of our times—swimming in the brine of that one eternal orbit—

suspended—

Parsons is unapologetic about Texas and the role that Texas plays in his poetry.
Many of his poems reflect that affection, but they do it in an illuminating way
that makes us go back and reexamine our initial perception. The most obvious
example is the poem "Texian" (a poem presented at the dedication of The Lone
Star Monument and Historical Flag Park in Conroe). One of the best examples is
the poem "Blinds," which starts off with the leading note: After John Graves's
Goodbye to a River.

Goodbye to a River is one of the keystone books of Texas. It details one man's
journey down the Brazos River before its flow is restricted by dams and flood
control. It is a story of discovery and self-awareness. Parsons's poem acknowl-
edges that wisdom that can come only from experience.

. . . I
am, also, a witness

and citizen of the ancient
tribe, that coalition
that exists in the universal

chain of fear

and food—the aiming

eyes behind our many

individual stands—

all narrowing our sights,

those many-faceted irises,

eyes we see through—

not with.

Parsons is a semi-retired empty nester. He and his wife, a fine artist, live in

Southeast Texas. He continues to teach writing and he is working with Wendy

Barker, poet-in-residence at the University of Texas at San Antonio, on an an-

thology of poems from the 1960s. In addition, he participates in annual cele-

brations involving the works of Walt Whitman and Emily Dickinson.

One of the poet's lines says,

"I believe it to be

unlike any other

conveyance . . ."

This easily could speak to the level of quality of Dave Parsons's work. The poems

contained in this book will elevate and transform you. With this volume the

Texas Poets Laureate series triumphantly continues.

Alan Birkelbach

Editor, The TCU Texas Poets Laureate Series

I

Poems from *Editing Sky* (1999)

EDITING SKY

I can see you there at your place
on Great Oaks Parkway,
a ten-year-old half-breed boy
all barked over in seventy-five
years of skin. You are writing me
the letter about living and dying,
cancer, and the new medicine men,
they're cutting you all up, and then
the bloodless scalping.

I think of our Apache mother
rubbing you raw with whitewash & pumice.
In trying to bleach herself out of your
smooth tailored skin, you became an even
redder half-Irish. Even before then, blood
had welled 'round your high cheekbone firmly
pressed to the hardwood stock, lightly butted
with the single shot from a small bore
Twenty-two. Your first buck's last leap

for that little space of blue between
Spanish oaks clinging to the hill country
roll brought you both down to earth.
Like some men, trees edit what we know
of the sky. A great oak is falling reaching
to steel crutches in its reaching
from the steep grassed banks
of Barton Springs to the other side.
You would know the tree.

It was our place by the deep: a cold, dark
blue hole in the fault line, the source
of our being there. One day we took turns
diving to see how close we could swim to that gush
of silent thundering. Then we would burst
to the surface gasping for the means, our
bodies spring-blasted, a tingling, newbornish sting.
Like survivors, we would crawl out under our tree
and lie like bacon on the sun-pebbled walk, dripping

while I hoped for one of your stories
about Indians, being a G-man, just anything.
I would then climb up to ride that smooth
saddleless girth, before it was packed with cement,
pretending I was Indian, too. I don't think you
ever knew how hard I rode that old tree
never reaching the other side. Today, if I could
I would leap up, straddling that gnarled,
crippled old steed—

borrowing God's spurs like stars,
we would buck loose from the earth.
Then picking you up out of that blanket
of skin, sleek we would ride—high—

ride the bark off that old paint
clear to the other side. Then
just as that fickle spring's reflection
began cooling off the sky, we three—
we would dive—

AUSTIN CHILD

I did not call you again tonight.
Again tonight, like so many times

since I have been gone from your nights,
I thought of you as you were years ago

on that last April evening,
your blondness sleeping curled

around cordless air in a small hug of self.

I had hunted softly your bed
by the window, above Walnut Creek.

On bedroom carpet-knees bending,
hostage hands behind me, I trailed

the gamy smell of five-year-old
to breaths as a fluttering moth—

mirroring beats, mirroring beats—

finding you without touching you,
missing you two weeks at a time,

all part of a strange ritual of measured
loving, in which we monks of infinite

resignation lay awake without calling
while my child in Austin sleeps. . . .

sweat of sleep humidifying my mind.

MEMORIES OF CAMP MATHEWS
IN FINNISH RHAPSODY

To be a Marine, you must love your rifle
for a while, at least until you are free
of Drill Instructors, the keepers of the truth of death.

And while you are in this dark state, a boot in boot camp,
you will pray for war every evening, desperate for a fight,
a reason for this purgatorial tie, a proof.

During the scorched inland days, the California summer
skies are rifled with reptilian eyes, sights narrowing
a simple human form, a symbol that could be a child's

sketch of his father or brother, any mother's son
springing up before you, a rapid-fire target
with no discernible face, the face of us all.

LIFEGUARD

We can agree to the memories
of brutalizing fireflies
in our own unique and sinister
ways. And the smell of chlorine
on the dry chafed skin is the same
in the summer saunas that were
my Austin and your St. Louis.
You have your long vacation days
in your pedophile neighbor's guard-less
pool, blurred in your memory,
like peering through a panic-fogged mask,
after being held down under the water,
under the years—reminds me
of my endless longing for someone
to save on the many sleepy days
of lifeguarding Barton Springs.
Those deep, cold, clear waters
that brought me the hot hippie girl
swimmers tugging at my drawstring
mind with their long well-kempt bodies, breast
and buns aching sun, shortening
the hours of light and cool

evening baseball games at Disch Field;
and ice-cold watermelon stands,
with a touch of salt for the tongue,
as bare, tanned damp legs dance
that lusty music-less tune under
the green picnic tables on the hard
dry dirt floor; or the evening, Rusty and I
hid Lone Star beer and Juicy Fruit gum
in a Scarbrough's shopping bag,
and giggled like girls into the Paramount
Theatre balcony to watch some long forgotten
screaming horror movie, only

to get kicked out by an usher, when
an empty bottle got away—time
rolling down the concrete stairsteps,
each step
sounding
an agonizing
report of loss.

Gone are those lost moments
at the Big Chief Drive-In, watching
Doris Day fantasies while squirming
around on the sweaty vinyl seat covers,
contorting within the shelter
of our own man-made fog
around the transmission hump,
the snare of pedals, strange
zippers, buckles, clips, and the damn
gear shift knob—

Buddy Holly was sweet in the air
of almost everything in between.
All summer fire and glorious
memories to me until
I think of you and those cruel dark
voids of yours, the blurry depraved
pool, that private swimming hole
without a guard,
that you must dive back into, time
and time again, but now, know
you are not alone.

THEY

Now that we know that Harry has Alzheimer's
we catch ourselves wondering out loud

about our own memories, searching
for that small void in our understanding

of time's continuum. This cruel wound
that delicately as some evil surgeon unseals

the mute gray bindings that hold
ineffably the inventory of a life,

stuns us again and again with horrific wonder,
leaving us with facial expressions, not unlike his,

as he turns his bent spade, again and again,
like some blind farmer through

the rough weed-filled furrows
of recollection and recognition.

At the Garden Café, Ruth stately still,
rotely asks him in that wifely way:

Would you like tea or coffee, Harry?
Harry, do you want tea . . . or coffee?

. . . then the realization . . . *oh . . . oh, give him tea.*
An acquaintance happens by the table,

and Ruth graciously, dutifully introduces her
to Harry, who, as always, smiles affably

and responds, *I am not really here,
you know*. Later, I accompany him

to the men's room, where he becomes confused
and begins to wash his hands before entering

the small dark stall with its endless
roll of blank white sheets of paper.

Standing before the sink, he stares
with what appears to be rapt erudition into the mirror

and whispers in that familiar, gentle fatherly tone,
He wants to come back, you know; he wants to come back

and they—they won't let him.

comforter

After turning out the lights,
you curl under the comforter

away from me, as I settle in
behind our half-curved legs.

We are pieced together:
halves of a mid-November moon,

our bodies, an echo—
giving—receiving—yearning

from the vague middle
among thoughtless glands,

as our feet try each on
in the twisted play of loose ends—

loose connections making & breaking
the clumsy vows of dumb extremities.

I remember our children—hugging
their small truths, the war realities

of stuffed animals, the silk of their young lips
against the smooth blanket bindings . . . safe,

complete.

In the morning the auburn of you orbits
to my bedside and softly descends

with the foggy aroma of ritual tea
or Colombian coffee, falling through

my squinting ellipse, somehow adding
to what seemed complete in that darkest

of patterns. These are not memories
randomly reasoned, nor the flawed promises

made by fickle limbs. These are a few
of the star stitches that burn in the bunting:

a gilded bit of the fabric of what we were,
what was saved without being chosen, folded

neat at the corners, our mellifluent patchwork.

re-resurrection

When you began the series of endangered species posters
I could think only of that yellow bore of *National Geographic*,
its four-colors bleeding periodically to death, taking thoughts down
that endless earth line that always returns to where it began.

The old cookie canister tin between your legs that held the fuses
of color, stayed crotch-hot as I laughed at the irony
of animal crackers parading around the volley, as
if in celebration of your passion, unaware we had
eaten their bread-brothers, biting their heads off first.
An arctic fox in snowy-eyed wonderment
followed a prairie chicken's
moldy orange strut
through the gray
tumbles.

Then
after you'd penciled
that ridiculous brown pelican proud,
that the eagle came—

re-resurrecting
the thoughts of them—
fellow Marines
I could not live without
sixteen years
dead.

SOUNDING

Tonight, three gray whales are bobbing for air,
feathering up through centuries of ice,
chanting toward the light shades of shadow

that mark a ragged, scarring circle of sky.
Television tells me that one of the three
ghostly figures is very young, perhaps a son.

I click the set off,
and I move from Point Barrow, Alaska,
to our kitchen, the last muted sounds

of the ceiling fan's circling fades
from the living room, drowning
in the omnipresent silence—I think of my children

all sleeping as I left them, curled around
cordless air in small hugs of self—looking
down into the sink, my face mutates

in the reflections of stainless steel—
like opening my eyes under deep, clear water
and finding some twisted, familiar face

staring back. Turning on the tap, I wait
as the small round light at the end
where the only sound

is the predictable exhaling escapes
and the inevitable gushing falls
to the draining . . . to a larger dark.

The heated water kicks in—emerges
blunt—a subtle change in pitch: a fission
born by quickening of atoms—that tiny life.

A sound so slight as to have been lost
to me the many years before this very moment.
I have heard it said that sound, once born,

swims in air immortal, circling
within its own sphere of existence,
bobbing through timeless atmospheres

that are deep and clear, like some holy water—
atmospheres that hold the spawning tympanum
of every faint first breath, every straining lonely

last gasp and every mourning parent's gnashing, "No!"
Standing in the center of this simple kitchen, for the first time
in over forty years of my sloping for light—I am certain

Truman was wrong, we were wrong, and the horror for me
is the equal certainty, I would have made the same decision.

GOOD FrIDaY

I

I am thinking of my sister Patricia
this Friday before Good Friday,
as always, her brown moon eyes rising
out of another year's memories, falling
into the slow contemplations
that circumscribe my thoughts, memories
that must be reviewed like some celestial truth
every Holy Week.

According to my mother,
at eight years of age Patricia
was the brightest of we four children.
I imagine her eyes then: the snap,
the spark they must have shown
anticipating Easter weekend.
Northcross Shopping Center
was within sight of our backyard
across the vacant spring field
of milkweed and scrub grass
that was to soon become
Lamar Junior High's playground.
We had made the trip across the field,
running across the busy Burnet Road
countless times.

Y'all hold each other's hands and look
both ways before crossin'. . . you hear me, David?

I don't know why I didn't go with them
to buy Easter candy that Friday.
I cannot recall the sirens or how
I learned of the accident. I only remember
being on my knees at the foot
of my parents' bed, praying
the prayers of a ten-year-old
for the life of a little sister,
making promises I could not keep.

She was in a coma for months,
after three brain operations,
she was still not expected to
survive . . . a part of her didn't.
They always said that it was the rocket
hood ornament of a fifties model Buick. . . .

II

Good Friday gray mutes
veins of red and green: stains
of the glass butterfly
that floats in the corner
of my bedroom window.
Nancy says that Good Fridays
are always overcast, cloaked
in gray; that Easters end up
bright and sunny. It pleases her
to think of these days as being arrayed
as her priest: auguring those days
of blood and sun. . . . I am thinking
of my sister, Patricia, she is crossing
the vast green field that separates
our home on Shoalwood Ave. from the busy
Burnet Road and Northcross Shopping Center;
where the Big Bear Supermarket holds
the visions that are a child's Easter, where
the flesh of eggs is always marshmallow sweet,
their hard white shrouds arrayed colorfully
in the habits of make-believe seasons
and chocolate bunnies with their dark hollow heads

wait like their many blood-filled brothers: stilled
on the center stripe of the high traffic shopping lanes,
frozen by the flashing silver eloquence of midday grills
and windy mechanical groans, their hollow heads
destined to know in an horrific instant everything
about teeth and chrome.

III

Nancy's prophecy is fulfilled: the stained glass butterfly
is floating in the bright bliss of a blue Easter sky.
I envision my sister, Patricia, in San Antonio
in her small apartment, feeding breakfast to Bela,
her two-year-old daughter, her miracle child.

Patricia and her doctor had believed Bela
to be a reoccurring kidney ailment. After all,
Patricia was well over forty; thought to be barren
because of the months of darkness—she was six months
pregnant . . . my mother gasped over the telephone,

David, it's a miracle of God!

Three months later Bela was born . . . on Good Friday.

This Easter sun will fall into the surviving pines
that stand like stoic pedestrians across my driveway.
With unabiding glee of a child's first enlightenment, light
will breach the skull of the earth, parting, imparting,
rootless, wonderful spontaneous laughter throwing
an enlarged silhouette of a butterfly onto the pillows
of our bed, where later, my own earth-brown iris will fall
and then rise, darting across an airy field, trying
a kind of sky, with this young blush of light
dotting that darkest of paths.

canoeing

I

Moving a canoe to water
is hands-on and awkward.
I remember teaching
canoeing
to the Boy Scouts
of Camp Tom Wooten,
where Bee Creek
finds an Austin lake,
boys wrestling aluminum
wedges, plowing crooked paths
to slippery slices of water,
obliquely reminiscent
of an old woman
moving through her beads
to the smooth, flat surface
of the cross,
making Earth's ending
a physical release.
Reaching the longer water
requires centering ourselves:
balancing belly-deep
among larger ribs
than any
Adam.

II

Like the Hopi Indians, we
have our water clans,
yet, our being
is not found
relived
in the reversing
symbols of clouds.
Nor will the schematic
of our past
be discovered, charted
mottle-brown

on some slow moving
hawksbill.
We walk on the wet sand
between the sounding
blue
and the dark
wood
at the foot
in the shadow
of the mountain.
Between the ark
and the armada
the mechanism
of the arm
is defined,
the oar locked
arms of
men.

III

Entering
the water
I found the wisdom
of forms, the giving
and the taking
of bodies
without the torque
of metal
or the tourniquet
of wind—
the way odd
shapes slip
like oval thoughts
into our future,
making
unconscious & precise
the many decisions
of faith.

IV

Lying inside
a grounded canoe
at night, the cold face
of the earth feels
vague as a tumor
through the thin back,
where, like minds, the ribs
are worn
from the inside
out.
This night dreaming
from the overt corners
of a circumsectional
cocoon, sails me
solid as any
Mareotic Lake,
wine or sea,

takes me—
takes me—

from our dark
ellipses,
we all blink
stars.

II
Poems from *Color of Mourning* (2007)

color of mourning

She awakened to Texas summer bright
in her eyes, throwing on a new yellow
robe, she dragged her body into the kitchen
to make coffee which she dug from a deep
yellow decanter. Awareness steeps through
the heart beating perks, her eyes fall on the child's
drawing that was stuck on the refrigerator door,
a yellow duck swimming on deep dark
water under another bloody sun brimming
with amber iris—Iris, goddess of the rainbow,
adding to the litany of golden messengers, all
bringing to her mind the dress, the yellow
dress that she had given to her niece
for her fifth birthday, the sweet lemon
yellow dress that the child delighted in so
that today she was to be buried in it—the sanctuary
of the summer kitchen felt unusually cold
as she cracked a single egg, spilling
carefully the delicate yoke onto melting butter
thinking, yellow—yellow—
yellow should not feel like this.

AUSTIN RELATIVITY

The old flagship Night Hawk Restaurant sits at a memory axis—
just over the Colorado River Bridge where Riverside Drive crosses

South Congress running east toward the Bergstrom Air Force Base;
where, at the guarded entrance, the large painted water tank spouted

PEACE IS OUR PROFESSION, the home of Dr. Strangelove's
bombers of the sixties; and later, those chillingly beautiful aquiline

Phantom jets streaking over the emerald hill country rolls
in the seventies and eighties; this same road ran west past the lazy

hills of Barton Springs, where those stunningly free living hippie
sprites would play and lie topless, sprawled across the lush

north green banks . . . across from the icy blue pumping methodical
flow of the springs that fronted my guard stand, appearing

at times as bodies strewn like casualties of some insidious sun
bomb, as I sweltered in baby oil mixed with the bold blood

of iodine, squinting over small patches of zinc oxide, musing
to the radio sounds of the Stones, Dylan, the many varied

voices that pumped with steely laced drum beats a music
into the heart of our turbulent days, instilling an urgent urge

to physically act—to escape from the stagnant pools of our youth,
to dive into the current of whitewater energy of the times, swim

that dark and intoxicating mystery, that dangerous rushing, rushing—

IT'S NOT ABOUT REMEMBERING

The rare books were on the top floor
of the University of Houston's library,
a building that did not tower
and offered very few windows.
The Gentleman's Magazine offered the view
of England's news events, a medieval
Reader's Digest from which we of Rothman's
seminar were to glean the details
for a paper that would be a proof
of our proper awe for the curiosities
of the period, a report that is lost to me
now, though a fragment of the search
has revenantly appeared at odd
and unexpected times through
these many years—a small news item

    beside the long list of timely
    and mostly untimely deaths: ox cart
    accidents, family ax murders, and the peculiarly
    high instance of suffocations caused by a swelling
    of the celebrants' throats after swallowing unseen
    bees that had lighted without a discernible sound
    onto the froth of the goblets of golden
    mead, perhaps buzzing only as they delivered
    their stingers to the root of the dumb tongues
    in the dark red tomb of the throat
    where I imagine an odd death rattle duet
    echoing as bodies tumble and worlds change. There

beside these mostly timeless obituaries
was the report from Spain: citizens
from a small mountain valley town
had experienced a bolting earthquake
that was so severe their church perched
over a mile above had been totally destroyed
as witnessed by the sound of their famous
bronze bells playing the chaotic, melodic finale
as they rolled down the rough, dry gullet
beside the vibrant village green road
to that dark quiet, events reminding me
of that early December evening, sitting

bone-cold in those common high school
bleachers of what is now the Stan Slaughter Jr. Gym,
the clarity of that precise moment of silence
among the fleshy throng of pre-holiday cheer,
when Stan Slaughter Sr. could sit no longer sanguine
next to me, leaping to his feet to thunder down
the stadium seats to his fallen son, the undefeated
senior captain of the Blue Devil wrestling team, limp
in the arms of that dark referee, having broken his neck
to escape a first pinning in front of an athletic director
father and the stunned crowd, momentarily speechless
in the square confines of a single horrific thought, trapped
among the bees, and the bells, and the other dead friends.

orange county april 29, 2005

It is Friday and though I am over a thousand miles away,
I can see you clearly in the East Texas morning
rolling away from my vacant side of the bed
to your feet, as you are compelled
to do every early morning, moving
militarily through the mechanics—creating
another day: the first call of the toilet,
shuffling to the kitchen, water for the kettle,
the daily doling out of the medicine
to the white counter top, the orbiting shuttle
to our sleepy daughter's bedside
for the exchange of her pills for the small dog
curled resistantly warm under their covers—
And there you are . . . there between the oak tree
and the row of dogwoods doing dog duty on your birthday—
what are you thinking today? If I were there, with you
I would not know—behind the physical, the mundane
there is the wonder, the mysterious and unique impulse
that resides in the essence of you—the creation of stunning art
out of the dark world of your haunting subconscious—
I have rarely been able to guess those memories, those thoughts—
even if I were on that common quay—my face inches
from yours, falling, plummeting dizzily into the auburn
framed countenance of your glowing presence—tripping
into the folds of your graceful familiar form, fixed
in wonder on that onyx centering in the greyhound blue eyes,
where that ineffable chalcedonic entity resides and in some
oblique way, *takes dominion of all that surrounds.*

STILL LIFE

It is the day after
your seventy-ninth birthday
and I have been reading poems
by Billy Collins—the one
to the invisible reader
prefaced with the Yeats
epigram: *a poet . . . never*
speaks directly, as to someone
at the breakfast table—
perhaps, this has been the problem,

my many failed direct attempts
to write about you, to you, celebrate
or bemoan you, that Georgia
red clay realist you . . . cast
in grand lifelong romantic fervor.

Nancy has been painting a still life
all week, fixing an eggplant's
bold bruise to the blood of merlot
spilled into a single glass stem
beside three green apples.
I have been unable to pick
the specific fruits or wines
from your life-filled bounty
to place carefully on a page
where, the swell of the color
of a moment like my first
awareness of your intense individuality
might be reflected subtly on to egg-
plant skin of my skin—blood
of my blood.

speechless

I found my father that late December morning,
as if he had just lain down to sleep, hands
at his side, right hand holding his always present
asthma spray, dull eyes seeming to ponder the tiles above
as if absently looking for familiar shapes to pass
the time, like he taught us to do with the clouds
on those long, infrequent West Texas road trips.
He would take us for a week or so, to allow
Mother a summer break and help us to understand
a rag salesman's life without having to actually speak.

I found my mother after penning a poem articulating
the difficulty I had experienced writing about her—she
was kneeling, dressed for bed, into her small glowing
bathroom tub that received her petite frame
like a large porcelain sea shell with its life half in—
half out—her face pressed flat to the surface, as if
she were listening to some astonishing sound—blush
of crimson whispering from her mouth—nothing
in her entire life ever could keep her speechless.

AUSTIN FIRE

*Memories from the day of the University of Texas Tower shootings
and the 100th anniversary of Scholz Beer Garden on August 1, 1966*

Out of the cave
of European History class
I am struck
by squinting bright skies
strolling on the edge of the shadow
of the university tower shade
through the southeast campus quad
flip flopping to my Mustang
for my short drive to work
less than an hour before
student victim #1
will fall
in that very path.

I am traveling back now—
back to the pool—
down the hot tar entry
down the pebbled walkway
to Barton Springs
churning shadowy deep blue—
it's the blues—the gushing
blues 68 degrees year-round
offering a deadening numbness
making the youngest of skin
cadaver cold and this ordinary
workday, I am just another life-
guard cut loose too soon.

And now—again
I am driving back
again back and away
away from the many
oblique precipices—falls
hidden undercurrents
jutting stones in the blinds
of the limestone aquifer
traveling back under and through
the towering pecan trees
just a short dash—and now again
Barton Springs Road—
The Rolling Stones—*Can't Get No*
Satisfaction . . . everything
is heating up the day.

At Scholz Garden
another grand spring
100 years of beer flowing
unjudgmentally through
the many unruly seasons
through the untold
joyous and unfettered
the anonymous generations
of the deemed and the damned
and all their wagging
Did you know(s) . . . flying
around the ever blank
pages of air—air that receives, never
recording a single loving or gnashing word
of the produce of this imperfect garden
those sweaty hound dog days—I feel
that very air here again now—the gamy
smells of the Dutchman's beer garden
the carefree summer women
laughing braless in loose tie-dyes
swilling nickel Lone Stars
aiming flirtatious glances
then firing their deadly frank stares
swinging suntanned legs

to the jukebox beats
Hey, Mr. Tambourine Man
play a song for me . . . all
positioned between
the two towers: the Capitol dome
topped with Lady Liberty
and UT's apex and bastilles of education
and there now . . . and again—white puffs—

Sniper! Sniper!

Girls first! diving under
stone gray concrete tables
towering turquoise sky
ragged clouds
ripping the battle blue
drifting . . . mist-like . . . hiding
momentarily gunsight portals,
and our shade tree bunkers
fiery memories
embedded
like so many stray shots—

He was a crew cut
every mother's son
Boy Scout—Marine
sharpshooter
again all paths of mine—
In his last note to the world
Charles Whitman
requested an autopsy
with special consideration
to his brain . . . they found
a tiny, cloudy gray mass
of malignant tissue lined
in crimson—seems it's
always the smallest of embers.

NIGHT HAWK

Congress Avenue rolls south from the Paramount Theatre
straight through sentries of live oak over the Colorado River
before it was a lake—

over that first main bridge before it housed the dark cloud of
bats and past the flagship Night Hawk Restaurant, where I
remember

running head to chest into President Lyndon Johnson as
his Secret Service agents, holding the glass doors open,

looked on in horror at the unexpected possibilities
of our collision, as I swung into the double doors

like some unexpected and inescapable event in Asia,
from the snaky nook of the restroom corridor, unaware

of his incoming entourage—*s'cuse me—no, pardon me!*
For a brief moment we did that uncertain dance to squeeze

by each other in the small vestibule of the double door entry,
LBJ in trapped composure, I imagine, with steak or a beer on
his mind—

I—in awkward and puzzled wonderment—Secret Service agents
on the outside and inside doors—staying stiffly cool—sizzling—

challenge court

In the Challenge Court you have no set partner
and the matches come to you like blind dates

with their many unexpected quirks: odd
styles of service, surprise shots and strange

nuances that bring mystery and a certain
edgy anticipation to every game. It is there

that I often found him with his ex-Marine handshake
and congenial look-you-in-the-eye smile . . . before and after

our play. He was the gentleman hunter—when you
became his game, his style was a kind of stalking.

I remember my old Austin friend and partner Jim Sellers
with his awesome animal athleticism—relentlessly attacking

the ball straight on with stunning velocity, as if it were
some huge and lethal insect, swatting it time and time again,

anticipating its geometric flight like some expert entomologist
gone mad, most volleys ending in dramatic and resounding

bottom board kill shots, whereas Fred's style was as smooth
and confident as his demeanor and his ageless pompadour,

only with fisted waves, curls, and left hooks—deceptively deadly
and yet, not extreme, not like "Captain Hook" Reeve, with his jaw-

drop—ball hopping, Fred's way was subtle . . . like some cancer
that after being diagnosed in the first prophetic shots brought pre-
dictable

and deadly ends to the remaining volleys. That one such as he,
with such control, was downed with that single shot to the heart

is not ironic, there is no poetry to our loss—there is only the stillness
of that quiet valve: the Handball Challenge Court—waiting—

in the downtown YMCA in the heart of Houston's tangle
of arteries and the question that comes to mind every time

I now stoop through the small passageway to begin
another challenge match: How could a totally empty

20 x 40 x 20 room with white walls seem more vacant?

THE PRIDE

Running with those young lions so many years ago offers up
memories of each that are ineffable . . . their individual aspects
are wound around in me—timbres of song—ruddy Swede, tough
as a fence post; mythic storyteller Terry's infectious laugh; Steve
with his strutting bravado and his Flip Wilson smile; lumbering
Robert, a Saint Bernard in another life; and brilliant Jeffery John's
tall and angular Cherokee presence—I cannot pen in a single line
the unique aspects each imbued in a single line—each deserves an
    entire poem,
odes that when chased, escape into random memories—fragments,
    like

those countless Austin summer evenings, we would all cram inside
    and out
of our group troubadour Rusty Wier's El Camino (he named Tom) . . .
    it was our
weekend ritual of cruising like sharks from the Holiday House on
    Barton Springs
Road south to the Pig Stand, across from the Austin Theater on South
Congress to peruse each hangout for whatever was happening . . .
always on the prowl for a carnal teasing glance—a fresh glowing new
face—blond pigtail—laughing into a Coke and fries, or the other
testosterone rush of some rival's challenge framed in a car window
glare—as we would glide by—their orbiting tail fins crouched in
chrome—glaring red—a ritual that has become an American pop
culture cliché, and though we long for that animal quiver that always
triggers the nostalgic images so intricately meshed in memory with
those pyrotechnic sounds: Buddy Holly, Elvis, The Stones, The
Beatles, The Eagles, The Beach Boys,
Simon, Garfunkel, Peter, Paul & Mary, Motown—the list just keeps
humming—

We can't deny the outrage of it all: the Pollyanna idealism that took us, in less than
a score of rockin' years, from what seemed to be the hard-earned clarity of a proud
Ozzie & Harriet society to blurring interventions—changes that questioned all
that seemed settled by the mid-fifties; changes that even brought into question
the validity of all questions—there is in Africa an exotic magicicada species
that transforms itself every seventeen years—the number of years seems odd
and a bit arbitrary—their tymbals bringing forth a unique and wild new song, music
that, on a long summer night, is said to fill the trees; and after one listens for a while,
these sounds, resonating in a single chant, singing the haunting voice of the sacred.

VIEW FROM THE CLIFFS

Nature is a Haunted House—But Art—
a House that tries to be haunted.
      Emily Dickinson

At Timber Cove Inn, two hours north of San Francisco, the raccoons
come to our window after a swim in the rocky garden pools at sunset

and peer into our balcony window from the old oak tree that is twisted
and flailing away from the windy sea. They are looking for handouts

from the untold treasury of travelers: scattered pet food, an orange,
    perhaps
a scrap of salmon jerky—the air is crisp and rich with that nice
    mixture

of the bounty of human creature comforts in our encampment and the
    promising
poignant exotic ocean, blowing in its salted and measured breaths,
    offering

its own stoked and smoky light, light—bringing our polluted city
    minds
that sumptuous meat, the essentials for that hungriest of animals—
    Art.

In the mornings sleek abalone divers can be seen in the shallows far
    below
undulating like innocent seals fishing the jagged cliffs, spooning the
    rocks

for that other sweet meat—a month from now we will read news that
    one
of these morning swimmers will have lost his head to a great white
    shark—

Emily Dickinson said that a poem should take the reader's head off—
today, where the near crags drop off to the deep Pacific all along
    Highway 1,

great shadows are turning cold blue tones black and swirling like
    hunger
in its haunted aqua house, while a thousand miles away, in a
    makeshift studio

on the edge of the Big Thicket, an artist trades her years of working to
    capture
the blurred past through Realism for the oblique certainty of the
    Abstract, diving

again and again into her Dantesque childhood darknesses, finding
    red renditions
and stunting yellows, black and the uncertainty of gray—she is
    swirling the many

colors of the truths that had been too raw to capture on a canvas . . .
    previously too vivid
for memory's chaste channels, fits of splashing colors, violently
    invading the sweet

sublime of unconscious pretense—finding not *Paradiso*—but, a kind of
faith—applying the simple earthly tools of brush and fabric—
    fearlessly opening portals—

III

Poems from *Feathering Deep* (2011)

FeaTHeriNG Deep

After Edward Hirsch's
The Demon and the Angel

I believe it to be
unlike any other
conveyance

the manner in which
it carries us in
upon its own silence

the way an idea drifts
into the gray divide
where we find ourselves

in that sacred state—easing
quietly into the dark *duende*
to unconscious understanding

a lone canoe at midnight—blades
paddling deep—smoothly
and deftly feathering

that largest of bodies

Fire

After *Jo, La Belle Irlandaise (Johanna Hifferman)*
by Gustave Courbet

At first glance, Johanna Hifferman appears
to be brushing her stunning long red hair,
hair filling the frame as it forms her looming
intense face, where dazzling blue eyes blaze
into a handheld silver mirror, as the other
hand toils at fiery ringlets, petite fingers pulling
gently from atop the creamy painting of brow
above the magnetic passion of those eyes,
eyes drawing the looks of the crowded queue
all gawking like the awed bystanders watching
some grand building aflame, their attention
keeps returning to the two small windows, where
humanity might emerge, showing its true
face, some emotion, like fear, despair, desire,
lust, emotions they might all recognize within
themselves or their outed longings, all standing
like worshippers before some magnificent
cardinaled saint, like Joan herself, burning,
flaming . . . inside and out . . . all present—blessed
with fire.

EVENING AFTER EATING RAINBOWS
(CAUGHT ON MYSTIC LAKE)

A mostly found poem—for the Van and Kathryn Wood family

Bohumil Hrabal wrote that every beloved object
is the center
of a garden paradise
and everything that lives
must have its mortal enemy—
Lao-tzu said that to be born
is to exit, to die is to enter—
Rimbaud wrote that the battle of spirit
is as terrible as any armed conflict
and Kierkegaard said you cannot separate
the slimy from the golden fish
(without killing the fish)—
in a polluted river running
through stretches of factories
   a beautiful fish may sometimes
be found sparkling like an eye—

 Once a man collected books on aviation
   because he thought Icarus
was Jesus's forerunner—
   are we all like olives: only
when we are crushed
   do we yield what is truly
the best in us—
Inquisitors burn books in vain—if a book
   has anything to say, it burns
with a quiet laugh, because
   any book worth its salt points
up and out of itself—

When we were young lovers
          so transfixed
with the complexities, especially
          of the sensual body
we had to say everything
          with our hands
In the starry firmament of night
          the senses lie dormant,
an immortal spirit speaks
          in a nameless tongue
of things that may be grasped
          but not described.

After an evening considering all these found
          thoughts in your small body of fire,

I could easily coil inside myself
          like a cat in winter
but it is midnight and I am back
          on the outskirts of Absarokee, named
for the Crow, looking directly above,
          into the ebony wings of an unambiguous
Montana sky, my head arched up—
          and out—spinning—spinning—
in *Too Loud a Solitude*—

KITES

Death is such an awesome
experience that it takes
your breath totally away.

I wish for this poem
to be the antithesis, under
stated, even modest

like simply breathing,
yet, indispensable
like the brisk breezes

holding colorful sails
against clichéd blue skies
or the breath that sends

aloft the many shaped lively kites
like student aspirations, dreams
tied to the determined fists of hearts

with the almost imperceptible strings
of hope, perhaps one climbing a bit higher
with the small wind of this poem.

I wish this poem to breathe

Texian

Colonel Juan Almonte, Santa Ana's aide, was the first
To call his attention to the heralding of two golden stars
Floating in the familiar field of green, white and red
Over that unlikely mission fort Alamo, small stars
That foreshadowed the larger single searing symbol
Emblazoning our ultimate flag of Texas independence
We fly so proudly today. And each of the banners
That flew over those many battles, all spoke
With the same unwavering intonation, No!
No, we will not become minions! Imagine with me
The cacophony of these many varied accents,
Of Kentucky, Tennessee, Louisiana, Alabama,
And Tejano, lilting together in the casting throng,
A composition of the most unlikely of battlefield
Symphonies, a timpani for independence.

Walt Whitman wrote in his *Leaves*,
They were the glory
Of the race of rangers, matchless
With a horse, a rifle, a song, a supper,
Or a courtship, large, turbulent, brave,
Handsome, generous, proud, affectionate,
Bearded, sunburnt, dressed in the free
Costume of hunters, not a single one
Over thirty years of age.

These were the men and boys
Of whom Walt called the jet-black
Sunrise at the last battle Goliad,
The same ebony tinted sun that fell on
The hardened rough-hewn clay arch
Of the hallowed battlefield Alamo, where
Within the brawny breastworks of both
That simple chapel complex
And the ragtag men staged within
Were mirrored these same
Uniquely Texian traits.

Texian, Texian, Texian, the word
That soon returned a jet-black siesta
To the soldiers of Santa Ana
In the far-flung fields of beach brush,
Mesquite, live oak, and pines
Of the San Jacinto battleground,
Texian, a word immortalized
Now the world over
By the actions of these gallant few.

Yet, these were seemingly ordinary men
With common everyday problems, desires, prejudices,
Fraught with human frailties, not ideal or perfected.
It is said that even General Sam Houston
Years before these momentous days,
Standing deeply depressed perched
Top deck on the riverboat Red Rover,
Was saved from a suicidal fall by the sudden
Flash of auburn plumage as an eagle, a Cherokee
Omen foretelling a greatness to come, swooped
Auguring down toward him—

Today we stand with one of Houston's resurrected warriors
So perfectly formed by *Campobella's sword*, ennobled
Amongst these thirteen flags, not an hour's drive north
Of where his grand triumphant destiny brought us ours,
Where the wafting fragrances of salty gulf coast breezes
And the pungent smoke of gunpowder sweated the air
That breathed life into the fledging hopeful breast
Of a stately body to come, making legend these hallowed
Winged emblems now fully realized, as our omens,
Their bright feathers forever woven with the blood
Of these many iron-willed, unique, soulful
Menagerie of men: these Texians.

BLINDS

After John Graves's *Goodbye to a River*

I too have languished
in the chill
of a deer stand
at dawn in wait—
watching for those
jeweled eyes

to wander through brush
land trees—sleek auburn
presences lithely moving
through the dawning
air, rich with the hot
stink of life, as

I huddled damp
in the steam of my
own heat, the bluing
cold of my rifling
dark on dark—in
the swirling shadows
of the last fading

of evening's many
deaths, slayings that
went without a report
I could discern
in my blind of artificial
trees, and yet, I
am, also, a witness

and citizen of the ancient
tribe, that coalition
that exists in the universal
chain of fear
and food—the aiming
eyes behind our many
individual stands—
all narrowing our sights,
those many-faceted irises,
eyes we see through—
not with.

THE PEOPLE

Though they became known as Comanches,
they called themselves Nermernuh *(The People).*
The Handbook of Texas

Their ancestors thought
the wild flying geese
to be red-eyed white
hounds harrying
damned souls across
the evening skies—

I imagine them standing
in a trancelike state—
seemingly dumbstruck
by the sight of the furious
flights of those many small
hearts beating ruby hope
against plumed breast—

not unlike small flags
flying in formation
behind some unnamed
leader who from afar
looks no different
than the last lagging
harrier waving wildly—

and here, tonight
those spirits fret about
me in midnight's bed
reading—vivid stories
of bloody raids against
the emerging white menace—
clouds of covered wagons—

each crimson episode
another of history's
many tragic tales
of failed preemptions—
the image of that wild gaggle,
so fluent of air and time, returning
again and again and again

the way the scarlet-rimmed
eyes of the past always

infiltrate our present—

HILLS

Driving to Silverton
from Durango, we
survived the mountains—
harrowing hairpin turns
and steep shoulderless
massif grades that plunged
us white-knuckled to
another hilly hairpin turn
and after an anxious hour
a tiny town, a camp
of dollhouses still far
below us, dotting
the valley like some
grand idyllic village
and in the late evening

I finished reading
The Darkest Summer,
a book mostly about Marines
of the Korean War
and how they survived
hill after bloody hill,
because the war seemed all
about the capturing of this hill
or that hill, and the intense cold
at the Chosin Reservoir
that caused their weapons
to freeze, so that when
thousands of Chinese came
in darkness surrounding them, they
could only toss hand grenades
down the hills or up the hills,
it was always about this hill
or that hill and the maps in
the map rooms of the generals

on both sides, these hills
all had numbers
and the numbers were piles
of other numbers and they
were like the piles of bodies
that were collected on both sides,
because they could not bury
them, because the ground was frozen
so they had to make piles of bodies
until they could blow a big grave
into the side of a hill to entomb them.

Warfare has always been intolerable
for the infantry, not like the wars I played
at over forty years ago, a Marine, never
actually capturing a fortified mount
or defending a crucial hill, just enough
war gaming in the barren California
mountains or recon-swimming icy mountains
of Pacific surf off the sands of Coronado Island,
to give me a small possible notion
of what another Marine "Grunt" might
have been feeling in actual combat,
and tonight, alone in my camper
in this scenic Colorado mountain
valley retreat, I cannot escape
those 1st Division Marines
of that historic battling flight
from the icy Chosin Reservoir,
their stories are frozen in my head
and as they were totally surrounded,
they are embedded in graying hills,
springing up in dark ambushes
of my thoughts; and I remember

my own Drill Instructor preaching, how
fire superiority can overcome any hilly
fortification, explaining how the 1st escaped,
because every Marine is a rifleman
and each time those Jarheads squeezed a trigger
a Chinese soldier went to the cold hard ground,
and I keep thinking that it must have been something
else as well, because they were so outnumbered
and it was so frigid, and there were so many, many
hills, there must have been something burning
deep in the valleys of the very essences
of their individual beings, some other kind
of unique fire superiority.

I WOULD GIVE YOU THE SINGLE STRAWBERRY

Not because it is the end of May: the season—
or that in the 17th century William Butler said,

Doubtless God could have made a better berry,
but doubtless God never did; or that the delicate

uniquely heart-shaped berry has been heralded
through the ages as a symbol of purity, passion

and healing; or because of Shakespeare's adornment
of Desdemona's hankie; or that Madame Tallien

of Napoleon's court would crush twenty-two pounds in a fine
basin and bathe in the glory of the luscious ruby juices;

nor because of its shape and color, it was the symbol
for Venus: Goddess of Love; or that it was widely held

by Romans to alleviate symptoms of melancholy, fainting,
kidney stones, halitosis, attacks of gout, liver, and spleen;

not even the legend that if you are lucky enough
to have a double berry and share it with one

of the opposite sex, surely true love will follow;
not even that they are the only fruit carrying their seeds

boldly on the outside like the regality of knights of olde.
I would give you the single strawberry as a kind of communion

offered in recognition, remembrance, and celebration of our
brotherly and sisterly spirits; moreover, as a reminder: strawberries
    are not harvested

with machines, their small bodies being so very delicate, human hands
must carefully harvest each berry; and as we savor it, let us meditate together
     on the visions

of the multitude of pickers—people like you and me—bending
under brutal sun in the rote of work, taking each unique berry

with measured grace, with reverent aplomb—I would give you
a single strawberry, because despite all that has perished

and been lost the past year, we
have lived to see . . . to taste another glorious spring!

THE MARRIAGE LOST

When everything that could fall

    has fallen

there will always be two hearts hanging

obscure, deep in the gristled harboring breasts

    of us hawks

floating in the constant wind of timeless memories, poised

in the heavy pewtered sky of our two minds—

    there is no true end

to this parting that we have lived with so many years

and now, like two intrepid birds of prey hunting

    in different territories,

we have in common our differences and the blood

of our blithely fey times together—still pumping wild

    in the deep craw

of the ancient machinery of the feathered crafting

of our individual lives since, and residing subdued—

    deep within me

endures the lofty vision from these high altitudes of a time— there

now . . . that small brown speck in your morning green eyes,

    eyes—

that with one blink of the thought of them, a bright portal opens,

a drumming heart—a catch of breath—still singing the sweet

                                    turbulent tones

of our times—swimming in the brine of that one eternal orbit—

                                    suspended—

stepdaughter

The term has always felt clumsy in my mouth
not unlike the relationship at its beginnings—

the tangle of diverse families that creates those awkward
first hugs—so full of the fire of mixed emotions—histories—

I remember the first time I was struck full face by the joyful
blue-green eyes that were plumed in that small face surrounded

by the shock of blondish brown hair . . . a stunning mane that seemed
much too substantial for a child's head—redolent of the thick, lush

texture of the mother's—hair that I remember hurriedly brushing
those early school mornings into shiny bouncing dog-ears—

stunning locks in complicated snares and rats, demanding gentle
concentration, occasionally evoking a snagging yelp and pain

reflected in those eyes—distinctive, subtly different from her mom's,
yet with the same unusual mesmerizing qualities. Those first blurring
    years

were the times the awkward nature of the term was truly onomatopoetic
of the relationship—countless hard encounters of miscommunications

and cobbling of minds and wills, and then euphoric discoveries—selfless
moments—genuine feelings of family—the years have passed and like
    roots

grown in buried tangles under a grand old oak tree, all those complicated
nerve endings, so raw from being torn from their original bodies,
    have found

their ways to firm new ground, rich loam—step . . . daugh . . . ter . . . the
term, as in introductions, still does not feel correct to my dumb tongue—
    my daugh . . . ter,

two smooth syllables combed together as two pigtails woven carefully
around each other—naturally: *I would like you to meet my lovely daughter,*
    Laura—

INSCAPING THE STORM

After Paul Mariani's *Gerard Manley Hopkins: A Life*

He once said to me, if the Christ
splendor had not seduced him,
he would have given himself
to the Lady Literature, his mind
to happily spin in the sweet Irish
gyre of his genes—his heart of mind
is still and forever will be pierced
by Gerard's grandeur, his body joyfully
churning with the oceans of inscapes
filled with blessed blood, propelling,
priming life's profundities through
the ardent aspect of a saintly eye,
and just as now, I remember him

standing tall on the very anniversary
of Hopkins's vows, a stormy Feast Day
of the Assumption, he is at the wheel
of the holy galleon, Sacred Heart Church,
and he—is—the eye in pandemonium,
like that bold lioness nun of the doomed
Deutschland, he centers himself
in the Mass, our majestic main mast
cloaked in the sails of his creed,
flying our colors proud, despite
the keening cancerous plague,
the waves of chemo nausea,
the agonizing baneful babble—all
landings within his sight fraught
with the wrecking rocks of ruin, yet
he stands amidst the brunt of it, his frail
alb-clad jib raised—strong on high, chevying
chaotic, chthonic born winds, proclaiming
against all darkness, to all above, all below
and to us huddled around on hallowed deck,

This is my body . . . this is my blood. . . .

Lake Lady Dancing on the Hill

Above the south shores of Lake Travis
she moves in the dawn that is breaking
over the railings of the house that clings
to the ancient limestone cliffs—she is the deep
and complex aroma of a dark, rich coffee held
in both hands against gusts of wind that have carried
a chill across the water, a body so deep and blue
that it captures all the light intense morning sun
can send against the hill country valley fortified
with green plumes of Texas plant life barricading
the giant furrow—the sides of the vast aqua catacombs.
Like that steady open vein that flows below, she will
be still moving in the evening that has broken over
that same ornamental ironwork for years, saving
the crow's watch of a porch that juts artfully from
the brow of the hillside she loved, she is this grand house
that will always bring joy to the hearts of memory—
to those lucky travelers that found themselves in her
respiteful inn of light and laughter for a day, or maybe
a weekend—for an, *anytime*—for she is the mother of joy,
she is the girl dancing and singing glory on the hilltop
high above the water that like her mind, looking so calm
on the surface, is always eternally sounding our depths,
she is that energy that makes all that surrounds resound.

knuckleball

We were a true blue baseball family.
Not that we didn't care for football or basketball,
we loved all the sports. The ritual begun by
our traveling salesman father, a former pitcher,
we would listen to the Yankees and Dodgers
on the radio—he loved Pee Wee Reese—and then
he would hit us ground balls in the front yard
on those slow hot Austin weekend days, the rare times
he was home from pitching Higgins Slacks on the road.

It was the only activity, I can recall, we did solely
with him—the single thing he would happily do
with us without a strong urging from our mother.
My brother Donnie was the best . . . glove hand magic
in retrieving the worm burners Dad would hit at us
from across the sidewalk that cut the yard in half
and often would give the ball an extra little hop
to be dealt with, as we would try to go to one knee
blocking positions, as he always coached us to do,
to make sure that if our hands were too slow or
we faltered in our judgments, our bodies would
make the stop—take the blow—thus saving a hit
to the neighbor's driveway or worse, the street
taking the ball down the steep incline of the hill
to the wild surrounding thick cedar country woods.

Our father never showed overt partiality to Donnie,
however, his body language and his hazel eyes gleamed
the pride in my brother's innate skills and though I think
our youngest brother Jerry was too young to perceive it,
I remember feeling a twinge in my chest, in the vicinity
of the heart, a painful plunk of envy, like one of those bad
hops—my father, he could throw a perfect knuckleball,
a deceptive pitch that comes at you surprisingly slow, vibrating
weirdly, creating an illusion of the ball's true path—true purpose—
I could hit his knuckleball—his best pitch—better than anyone.

TWO DOGS HOWLING AT THE MOON

I will always remember the last time I saw you,
at your *angel's*, Tricia's, crowded Plano townhouse,

and how, after our four hours of harmoniously
catching up on thirty some odd years of lost time,

I read you my poem "The Pride," about that pack
we ran with—we thought we were lions, we were

more wolves or stray dogs—reliving those old stories
of growing up together wild in the enigmatic sixties

in South Austin, like our tequila drinking contest
when I came home from the Marines, how I passed

out hearing you strumming to "Rave On," learning
later, you had quickly followed me to the darkness

falling dead-drunk onto your beat-up old guitar,
like some faithful warrior falling on his sword.

As our visiting ebbed, you played for me the second
of your three new songs, saying, *"I'm still writing—*

*can't stop doing that one thing—we're like those two
old dogs in my song, David, we writers just keep barking*

and howling at that ol' moon," your voice still
inimitably valved despite the chemo and the thousands

of songs poured out like manna to the many hungering
audiences of the nightlife you so loved and I remember

at that moment thinking how Li Po is said to have so
adored that great luminous orb that he perished, when

after a night of heavy drinking, he fell into the lake
attempting to embrace the dazzling antediluvian body, tumbling

headlong and alone into the deep ink of oblivion,
or perhaps, the masked reflections of an eternal light

and how you, after sailing through countless gigs
and seas of agave, one complimentary shot at a time,

were now arduously floundering to make the best of each
of these last painfully clumsy egregious moments,

like you always have, with that distinctive dancing
twinkle in the weathered squint of those smiling blue

eyes, eyes still fully alive in my memory, still dancing—

I suppose every human passion holds within its core
the germ of something lethal to its being and yet,

somehow, interwoven with the potential of rapture.
Tonight the sheer linen curtains of my bedroom seem

to be tossed by the blurring energy of the moonlight
bouncing glowing stones across the dark water of our pool

as the ceiling fan circles in its perpetual waving orbits
and I can hear my daughter's tiny lapdog underneath

my small dinghy of a bed gnawing like memories
on a T-bone scrap from dinner, he is at that phase

where all the meat is flayed away and one can only
hear the sound of bone against bone as he is working

into a rhythm in his ceaseless mastication, creating
his own unique kind of wild, raw, and satisfying music.

IV
New Poems

snapping in

*And already/nothing remains of the warrior but
his weapons/and his gaze.*
　　　Ted Hughes, *The Knight*

That is what my Drill Instructors called it, snapping
in, lying in the prone position for an untold time,

learning the nuances of integrating body and weapon,
arm tightly wrapped, trapped within the rifle sling's

noose, legs spread, elbows flexed into a natural tripod,
eyes searing through the narrow vortex of the battle

sights of an M1A1 gas operated, air cooled, semi-
automatic shoulder weapon, squeezing the trigger,

over and over and over and again, wishing for live rounds
to fire, hearing only the crisp jolting snaps of the firing pin

wondering, wandering through the dull soundless voids
of time and thought, occasionally finding melodic notes

of a kind of muscle memory, not unlike years later, standing
in the brisk cold waters of the Snake River, casting over

and over, and over into herds of galloping torrents, white
manes chaotically stampeding mountain stones and rainbows

and there—and there—and there, something wild, thrashing,
leaping ahead to a murky watery future, returning back, again

having no idea of the time that passes; when attempting
to move, numb, dumb legs, boots finding only slimy smooth

feral stones on the muted face of the yellowish green river
bottom, for an instant, the same hooked heart of the trout

in me flying from one element of air to another, and falling
rock hard, sniped, splayed body instantly awash in the icy, jolting

revelations that must eventually come to the minds of most all
falling bodies, that last flashing white epiphany—and then only

the sounding, drumming eternal waters, the steely tugging tow
of a destined time that must come to us all, of being snapped up—

THE ETYMOLOGY OF SOUND

There seems to be a discernable alteration, a variance
in the approaching sounds of a civilian helicopter,
and that of a life flight or a military craft, Black Hawking
into our psyche—piercing the very visceral essences
of our hunter-gatherer genes, that fight-or-flight instinct, adding
to our now learned tribal memories—guttural rasping blades
slicing through the jungles or deserts of any normalcy, chilling
us in an instant with the thought, something has happened, is about
to happen—heads up, heads down—it's in our heads, forever
now, in our heads, it's in our heads—

MY HERO COUSIN

He won no Medal of Honor,
the Distinguished Flying Cross
that does adorn his wall was not given
for one gallant and demonstrative violent action
above and beyond the call, as is often clichéd.
His Cross was received for the ten deployments
and the many scores of missions, flying
the jungled labyrinth of our national nightmare.

He is not returned and buried, too young
among the dead warriors of Arlington's
hallowed grounds or any other veterans
cemetery, though he is nearly buried alive
in the constant barrage of volumes of books
at the Brookhollow Public Library, where
he clocks in every day, again a volunteer,
now piloting tomes to precise landings
on the militarily lined maze of runway shelves,
with the same steady sure-handed manner

of the over three hundred missions he made
above those masked jungles of Southeast Asia
forty years ago, with his extraordinary relentless
patience, that unique unassuming heroic trait,
that joining of equal elements of all-knowing
wisdom and total ignorance, conserved
in the aerie catalogs of his mind, as certain
as all war's uncertainties, he routinely
climbed into lumbering C-135 tankers
refueling, renewing other fliers or the
mosquito-like FAC's (Forward Air Controllers),
guiding the lethal messages, missals sent
down by our fighter jets, daily doing his duty.

So much depends on men such as him,
methodically braving unthinkable possibilities
day after day, hours, minutes, seconds, their lives
checked out with the ever growing risk
of expiration, of never
being returned.

THE LOST GIFT OF TIME AND SIGHT

Most of the world is now watching
through a myriad of cold orbiting eyes.

I remember a time lost when there
was only the slow meticulous knitting

of the news, through the many
tellings and writings and readings

coming to us with the slow turnings
of the fabric of days, coming in orbits

of sun and moon, gifting us with time
to check the many stitches for flaws

made by the multitudes of tellers, carrying
on ceaselessly—but now cold aiming needles

like invisible missiles, piercing our airways,
our visions with missals of mayhem, ogres

of mind, invading our hours, days, blaring
screens, urging, hastening us to the precipice,

a cliff of mind, where lemmings leapt, finding
too late, the broken bones of cold, brutal truth—

FIGures

For Gene Antill (1935-2012)

When you walked into HISD's Contemporary Learning Center,
a fancy name for your last chance, and found yourself
in Mr. Gene Antill's class, perhaps it was your first real chance,
because when you found your face in the light of Mr. Antill's
visage, under those kind and twinkling eyes full of joie de vivre,
 you soon discovered that he knew you already, that you
were from the world of figures, figures like dropout rates,
learning disabilities, low test scores, and badass street bullies,
drugs, figures of missing dads and single moms with worn
worried expressions and no answers to the figures that you
have been unable to figure out, so here you are in Mr. Antill's room,
and you soon learn that here is a man who truly knows something
about the world of the numerous figures and here is a figure
of a man like no other, an individual that has figured out
most all those difficult figures—the hard way, by trial
and error, and here is a man that still, after years of figuring,
loves to figure the figures, a man whose infectious joy for living
a life in the world of figures radiates a hope that you can figure
it out, too, and he looks straight through you and sees nothing
but the possibilities of your figuring it out, for he sees the truth
you have always held hidden in deep in your gut and his easy figuring
of, and for you can only be translated into two figures, faith and love—

Archaic Relfections on Blake's Baptism

At St. James's Church in the heart of London
the ornate font is found as it was when it was cut
by Gibbons's sword, that likeness for the Lord.

Like the talc that is the clouds above England's
satanic mills, all come together church cold,
polished and still, and still I sit in wonder

of the Lamb and evil's carvings in the plan
as you must have queried at the end
of your first long night, after bending

thoughtfully down, in a love for the light.
Your last glimpse in rising might have been
the peaceful floating down of the dove,

but coming up and out and through the night
with a clutch of honed arrows, keen and quivered
gold, your sight wound round the tree of the font

to the end of the devilish curl, and it is there
where the head of a snaked darkness unfurled,
your mental flight surely must have sprung.

MY Previously owned son

I'll be watching you....
    Sting

Like me, and most of the men I know, he would wish
his poem to have a glib, self-effacing title, something
deflecting, as we all usually redirect any angst
that life might have or will befall us
with humor and; what our many pscho-
analyst family members would term,
stuffing it, and for him in the body of the piece
there must certainly be a musical reference
of some deep and meaningful nature,

after all, it is surely the sublime timbres of his mind
that have truly defined the essence of the young man,
and travel, perhaps a large ship, though not the Aggie
one, where he spent his first summer at sea, insearching
himself and other strange geographies, a discoverer—
yet, for him, it has always been about revelations

for the man I have been watching since the year
of his tenth birthday, when I first met full face
that smiling Dutch boy look of promise, pure, raw hope
and a palpable trust, despite all that he had witnessed
in his small version of the world. Years later, I remember

a face grown twice as old, in a hospital bed, the heart tests,
and we, having been told by the doctor, must inform him
of his grave and hopeless condition, and as we did so,
with our parent's acute agony, that same face stared
back at us with complete disbelief, saying, oh, that's bull
shit! No way! No way! And by day's end, we learned, yes,
in some miraculous way, the heart had begun to recover
as if willed so by the sheer power of his irrepressible hope,
inexplicably, creating his own realities and now, after all

these many years of watching, I know that my son's heart
is a unique instrument of music, with its own rhythms
and it is also a kind of boat that carries him and those
he loves, lifting anyone of life's many voyagers that find
themselves on his way, illuminating them, a turn of notion,
a portal to some strange joy that was a traveling embryonic
melody within the sacred valves of their own crafting of reality.

revenant OLD AUSTIN SONGS

I

When Chubby Checker's voice emerges again
resurrected from my oldies radio station
with that iconic first line invitation,
            Come on baby, let's do the Twist. . . .

it is again as the first time I heard it, and there
within are Jane Wolf and Kay Goodnight petitely
Twisting, Twisting, Twisting
taut teen bodies,

blond ponytails bouncing with the stirring beat,
at the Hancock Recreation Center's Teen Night, back
in a hot and gamy room crowded with gawking
adolescents seeing the latest dance for the first time,

having no idea that this moment was one of a beginning
of an era when the term *blow your mind* was the norm,
all jammed into one of the small rooms in my head, among
the many memories of those summer early sixties evenings.

II

When The New Christy Minstrels chime in velvet voices
so perfectly feathered together from my old LP,
Today, while the blossom still clings to the vine,
I'll taste your strawberries; I'll drink your sweet wine . . . there

is Patty's moon face floating timelessly below mine: flush
cheeks of pearl, our youthful sinewy limbs all akimbo, pungent
tang of college girl hormones—*I will feast at your table, I'll sleep*
in your clover who cares what tomorrow shall bring. . . .

another relationship like so many, many poems,
long published, and yet, for years, wrongly compiled, surfacing
in flashes, surprising jolts of emotion and regret, a raw chord
emerging off-key from memory's chthonic jaded catacombs.

III

When Carole King moans in her *Tapestry, So far away,*
why can't people stay in one place anymore?—I'm clinging
in stuttering rhythms again to ideal love—inimitable Terry,
our Austin stone split-level home hanging perilously

like a naive rock climber to the hillside of Walnut Creek,
the azure of the dark water swimming pool, suspended
like a dense watery cloud, sky on sky above hill country
live oaks, cedars, wild vines and scrub brush clinging

precariously to the crags below our bedroom window,
Bran-Cook's five-year-old feet doing that nightly dance
around the deep sunken pit of our airy vaulted living room
to our ardent young marriage bed, her childhood night-

time fears, so vividly realized in me now, her small pads
of feet, like some masterful sound technician bringing
that unlikely mix of nostalgic joy and regret, impossible
to safely separate, like the slime of some rare, splendid fish.

THE GUST OF WIND
A Landscape Painting by Gustave Courbet

Could this be Eden after the fall?
The great oak tree vacant of life,
living waters abandoned, mirroring

the dark blue mood of an angry God,
zealous sky flourished with the effects
of His last enraged pronouncement

a swirling black caped cerulean composition
casting His shadow over the small bit of light
that lingers, holding the remnant warmth

in the rocks that once gave them rest?
The sky is an aspect of an ocean, where
death commingles with life and even

castaway fruit is soon absorbed, adding
to that uniquely tart, fecund fragrance
of the inland sea's gusty birthing breath

of the many bold bodies destined to come.

acknowledgments

I wish to express my gratitude to the editors of the following journals and anthologies in which poems from this volume have appeared, occasionally in different versions:

Agave, a Celebration of Tequila Anthology, Borderlands: Texas Poetry Review, Concho River Review, descant, Gulf Coast, Louisiana Literature, New Texas, Numinous Magazine: Spiritual Poetry, SWIRL: Literary Arts Journal, Southwestern American Literature, The Criterion, The Langdon Review of the Arts, The San Pedro Review, The Texas Review, Touchstone Literary Review.

Poems from the books, Editing Sky, Color of Mourning, and Feathering Deep are printed with the permission of Texas Review Press.

My great appreciation to Daniel Williams and the fine staff of TCU Press for the gift of the Poet Laureate Series. I am humbled to be included. I also owe a special debt of gratitude to Paul Ruffin and the staff of Texas Review Press, who published my three previous books, inspiring and gratifying me. I have been extremely fortunate to have had the gifted editorial advice and friendship of Jean Wood and the many colleagues, mentors and friends; old and new, who have given me support, ideas and memories that have been instrumental in the creation of the poems for this collection; and always, my mother Reba Lanet Kierbow Parsons who turned me on to reading books one lonely summer in the rolling woods of Austin, Texas.

NOTES

EDITING SKY: Dedicated to James C. Kennedy

AUSTIN CHILD: Dedicated to Dr. Brandy Cook Parsons-Miller

MEMORIES OF CAMP MATHEWS: Where Marines were trained in marksmanship with a rifle.

LIFEGUARD: Disch Field, not to be confused with Disch-Falk Field, was located on Barton Springs Road, one block east of Lamar Boulevard and was used by the Austin Pioneers, a minor league team of the 50s and 60s. The field was torn down in the 60s.

THEY: For Harry Dazey

RE-RESURRECTION: Dedicated to the members of the Marine and SEAL training command who trained me at the Reconnaissance Scout Swimmer School at the Naval Amphibious Base, Coronado, California, later losing their lives in Vietnam.

CANOEING: The Mareotic Lake or Sea is site of the vision of the human soul in Shelley's *The Witch of Atlas* and appeared in Yeats's, *Under Ben Bulben*.

AUSTIN RELATIVITY: For the Barton Springs lifeguards of the sixties, especially Fred Hanna, Eddie Peterson, and Bobby Jones

CHALLENGE COURT: For Fred Copeland, lost to a heart attack at the Houston Downtown YMCA, Court 10

THE PRIDE: For Jeff Jamar, Terry Barnard, Bubba Johnson, Rusty Wier, and Steve Thompson

KITES: Originally titled "Occasion." The poem was composed at the request of the student editors of SWIRL: Lone Star College Literary Arts Journal, for their 2008-2009 issue, which they dedicated to me— a high and humbling honor.

TEXIAN: "Texian" was composed in response to a request from the City of Conroe and Lone Star Monument and Texas Historical Flag Park Committee, to be read at the opening, unveiling ceremonies on the 175th anniversary of the Battle of San Jacinto, April 21, 2011.

1. References to Col. Juan Nepomuceno Almonte were found in the *Texian Iliad* (University of Texas Press), by Stephen L. Hardin.

2. References to Sam Houston's encounter with the eagle on The Red Rover were found in *Sam Houston* (University of Oklahoma Press), James L. Haley's biography.

3. Craig Campobella is the sculptor of the statue of "The Texian" centered in the The Lone Star Monument and Historical Flag Park in Conroe, Texas.

HILLS: I am appreciative of Bill Sloan and his fine book *The Darkest Summer*, detailing the battles of the United States Marines that saved South Korea.

MARRIAGE LOST: For Dr. Terry Parsons Smith. The first line is taken from the Ted Hughes poem, *The Guide*.

STEPDAUGHTER: For Laura Doehrman

INSCAPING THE STORM: For Father Hubert Kealy (1938-2010)

LAKE LADY DANCING ON THE HILL: For Shirley Schwaller (1946-2007)

TWO DOGS HOWLING AT THE MOON: For my lifetime friend, Rusty Wier, an Austin Music Awards Hall of Fame songwriter with a double platinum song, "Don't It Make You Wanna Dance," that was included in the sound track of the movie "Urban Cowboy"

MY HERO COUSIN: For Major Richard Kierbow

ABOUT THE AUTHOR

David M. Parsons has been the recipient of a National Endowment for the Humanities Dante Fellowship to the State University of New York, the French-American Legation Poetry Prize, and the 2006 Baskerville Publisher's Prize from TCU for an outstanding poem published in their literary journal, *descant.* He holds six writing awards from Lone Star College System and was inducted into the Texas Institute of Letters in 2009. Parsons grew up in Austin, graduating from Stephen F. Austin High School. After graduation, he joined the United States Marine Corps Reserve, where he served as a Squad Leader in a rifle company and later as a Recon-Scout Boat Team Leader. He attended the University of Texas and Texas State University, where he received a BBA. After several years in business, advertising, and coaching basketball and baseball at Bellaire High School (where he was on the legendary Coach Ray Knobloch's staff that won the Texas State High School 5A Baseball Championship), he studied poetry with Stanley Plumly in London, England, after which Parsons entered the University of Houston Creative Writing Program, receiving an MA in Creative Writing and Literature. Dave Parsons's first collection of poems, *Editing Sky*, was winner of the 1999 Texas Review Poetry Prize and recipient of a 2000 Violet Crown Special Citation. He teaches Creative Writing and Kinesiology (racquetball/handball) at Lone Star College-Montgomery. He is founder and codirector of the Montgomery County Literary Arts Council Writers in Performance Series and chair of the Greater Conroe Arts Alliance. Parsons has four grown children and lives with his wife Nancy, an award-winning artist and graphic designer in Conroe, Texas. His website can be found at www.daveparsonspoetry.com